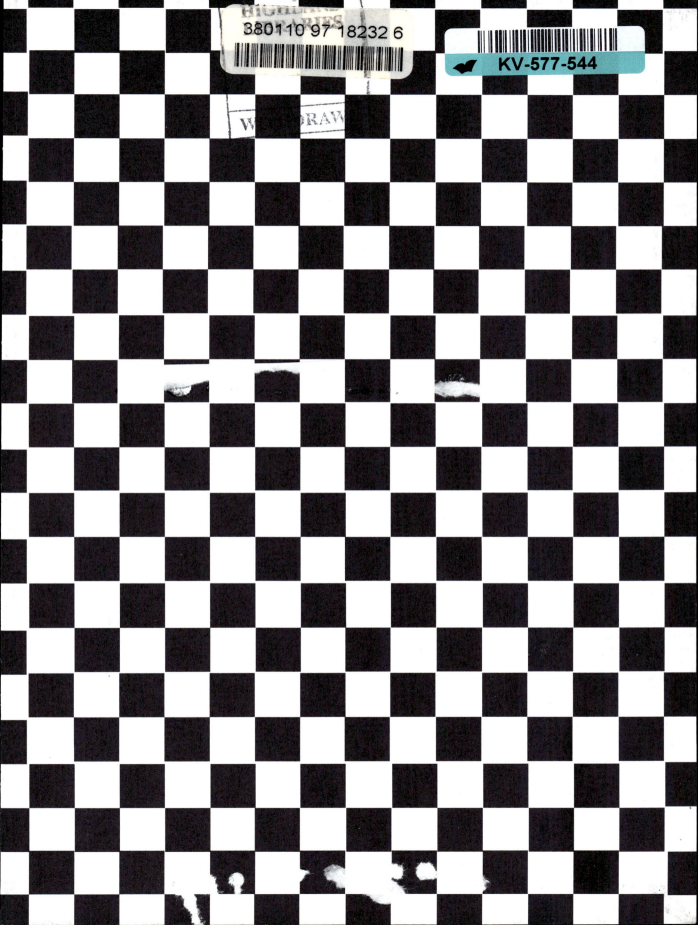

John Cooper is a geologist and Keeper of the Booth Museum of Natural History in Brighton. He has studied dinosaurs in Leicestershire and Sussex in England and at the Carnegie Museum of Natural History in Pittsburgh, USA. He is the author of several books concerning dinosaurs and has a special interest in the early history of dinosaur discoveries in Sussex.

Nick Hewetson was educated in Sussex at Brighton Technical School and studied illustration at Eastbourne College of Art. He has since illustrated a wide variety of children's books.

David Salariya was born in Dundee, Scotland. He has illustrated a wide range of books on botanical, historical and mythical subjects. He has designed and created the award winning *Timelines*, *New View*, *X-Ray Picture Book* and *Inside Story* series and many other books for publishers in the UK and abroad. He lives in Brighton with his wife, the illustrator Shirley Willis, and their son Jonathan.

Editor Karen Barker

Created, designed and produced by

THE SALARIYA BOOK COMPANY LTD
25 Marlborough Place,
Brighton BN1 1UB

ISBN 0 7500 2581 6

Published in 1998 by
MACDONALD YOUNG BOOKS
an imprint of Wayland Publishers Ltd
61 Western Road
Hove BN3 1JD

You can find Macdonald Young Books on the internet at http://www.myb.co.uk

A CIP catalogue record for this book is available from the British Library.

Printed in Belgium.

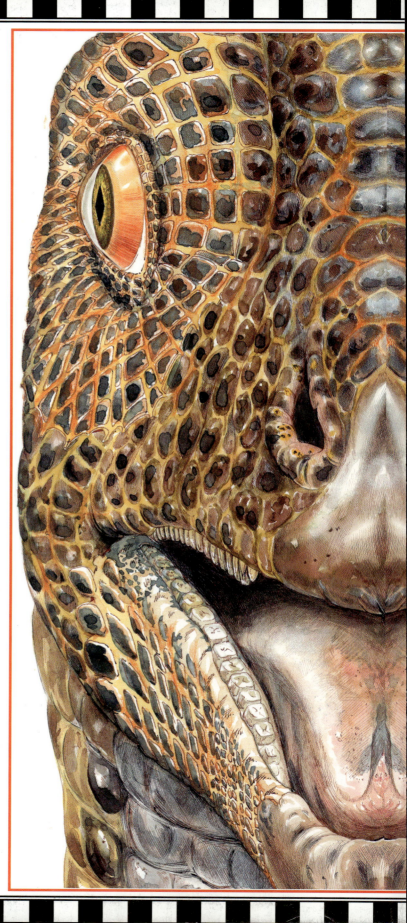

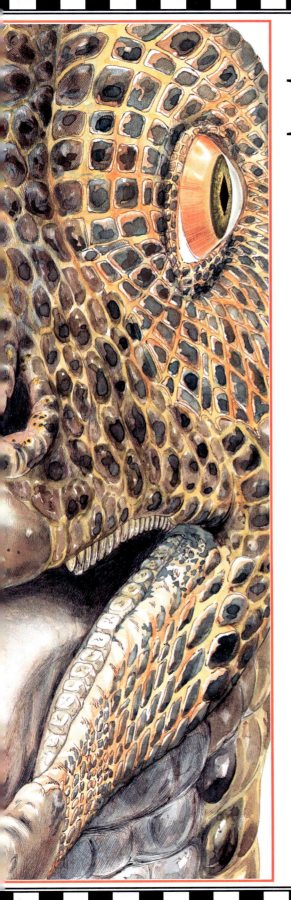

CHECKERS
DINOSAURS

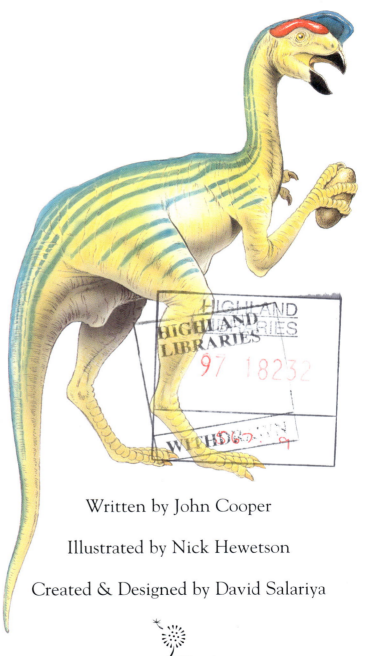

Written by John Cooper

Illustrated by Nick Hewetson

Created & Designed by David Salariya

MACDONALD YOUNG BOOKS

Contents

The age of dinosaurs

Dinosaurs were animals that lived during the Mesozoic era of the Earth's history – from 245 to 65 million years ago. They were reptiles, a group of animals which today includes lizards, snakes and crocodiles.

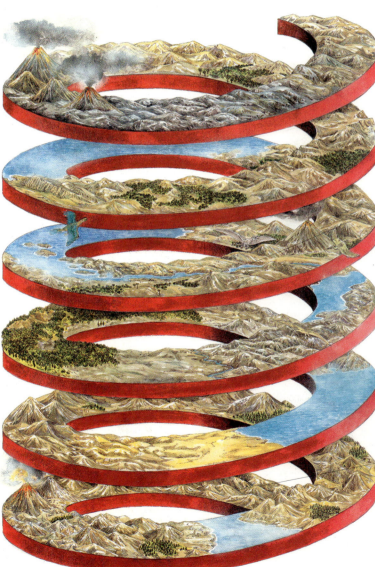

The Cretaceous Period

135 million years ago. The continents started to form the shapes we recognise today. The South Atlantic opened up and was soon followed by the North Atlantic.

The Jurassic Period

200-135 million years ago. The continents were splitting and seas divided the land.

The Triassic Period

245-200 million years ago. All the continents were joined together in a single mass – a supercontinent. Inland, the climate was very dry.

Modern fish, flowering plants and birds evolved. The climate cooled.

Many of the largest dinosaurs evolved.

Start of the Jurassic Period.

Dinosaurs were widespread across the supercontinent.

The world's earliest known dinosaur, *Eoraptor*, evolved in Argentina 225 million years ago.

Start of the Triassic Period.

What were dinosaurs?

Dinosaurs were not the first reptiles as many earlier ones lived before them. The remains of the earliest known reptile was found in Scotland in 1989 and lived about 335 million years ago. Dinosaurs only lived on the land. They were adapted for land-based life because their legs were held straight under their bodies like our own. These were good for carrying weight, for hunting with speed and for running.

A monitor lizard's legs stand out at either side of the body. The weight of the animal is carried by the joints within the body.

Diplodocus lived between 150-140 million years ago and was 27 metres from head to tail.

Pteranodon had a 5 metre wing span and lived 85-64 million years ago.

A pigeon has a 30 centimetre wing span.

The ancestors of the dinosaurs and some living animals like crocodiles became adapted for better strength and running abilities by evolving legs partly tucked under the body.

Deinonychus existed 110-100 million years ago and was about 3 metres long.

Stegosaurus dinosaurs lived about 150-140 million years ago and measured 6-7.5 metres long.

Modern crocodiles are 3-4 metres long.

There are a few familiar extinct reptiles which were not dinosaurs. Pterosaurs and pterodactyls flew, while ichthyosaurs and plesiosaurs lived in the sea.

Triceratops is an example of how dinosaurs had (and birds and mammals still have) their legs positioned directly under the body for strength and agility.

Dinosaur ancestors

Somewhere in South America, about 250 million years ago, a new group of creatures appeared. Evolution produced reptiles capable of racing swiftly on upright legs and capturing prey with specialised jaws and teeth – the first dinosaurs. Fossils of these first dinosaurs have not been found. But evidence of their descendants living only 25 million years later has been discovered. An almost complete skeleton of the world's oldest known dinosaur was found in the foothills of the Andes in Argentina in 1991. Named *Eoraptor* or 'Dawn stealer', it was only 1 metre long but would have been a fierce hunter.

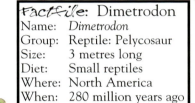

```
Factfile: Dimetrodon
Name:   Dimetrodon
Group:  Reptile: Pelycosaur
Size:   3 metres long
Diet:   Small reptiles
Where:  North America
When:   280 million years ago
```

This sail-backed early reptile had legs typical of slow-moving reptiles. Its sail contained blood vessels which could heat up quickly – helping Dimetrodon to become highly active for hunting – and could cool down when it became overheated.

Longisquama was a lizard-like creature from Asia and lived 240 million years ago. Long stiff scales covered its body and back. The wing-like structures may mean it could glide.

Eoraptor is the earliest dinosaur discovered. Scientists had long believed that the first dinosaurs were small, meat-eating hunters – exactly what *Eoraptor* proved to be.

The sleek and slender *Lagosuchus* had legs like a dinosaur and could run quickly to catch its prey. Some scientists think that it was the ancestor of all dinosaurs. The legs of *Lagosuchus* are typical of running animals. The shin bones are almost twice the length of the thigh bones.

Factfile: Eoraptor

Name: *Eoraptor*
Group: Dinosaur: Therapod
Size: 1 metre long
Diet: Small reptiles
Where: South America
When: 225 million
         years ago

Factfile: Lagosuchus

Name: *Lagosuchus*
Group: Reptile: Thecodontian
Size: 30 centimetres long
Diet: Grubs, insects
Where: South America
When: 250 million years ago

Early dinosaur catches the worm

The earliest dinosaurs entered the world of the Triassic Period, 248-213 million years ago. Then, the land was dominated by hot, barren areas. Only land near coasts and rivers could supply lush vegetation. While the plants provided food for a wealth of small creatures – insects, grubs, amphibians, molluscs and lizards – they, in turn, became food for the new and aggressive meat-eating dinosaurs. Although the first carnivore dinosaurs remained small, they were still at the top of the food chain. There is evidence too, of dinosaur cannibalism!

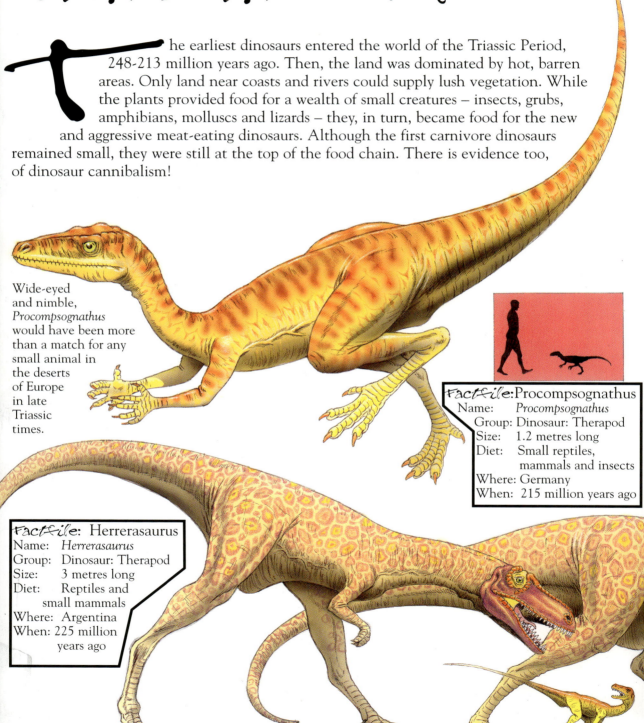

Wide-eyed and nimble, *Procompsognathus* would have been more than a match for any small animal in the deserts of Europe in late Triassic times.

Factfile: Procompsognathus
Name: *Procompsognathus*
Group: Dinosaur: Therapod
Size: 1.2 metres long
Diet: Small reptiles,
       mammals and insects
Where: Germany
When: 215 million years ago

Factfile: Herrerasaurus
Name: *Herrerasaurus*
Group: Dinosaur: Therapod
Size: 3 metres long
Diet: Reptiles and
       small mammals
Where: Argentina
When: 225 million
       years ago

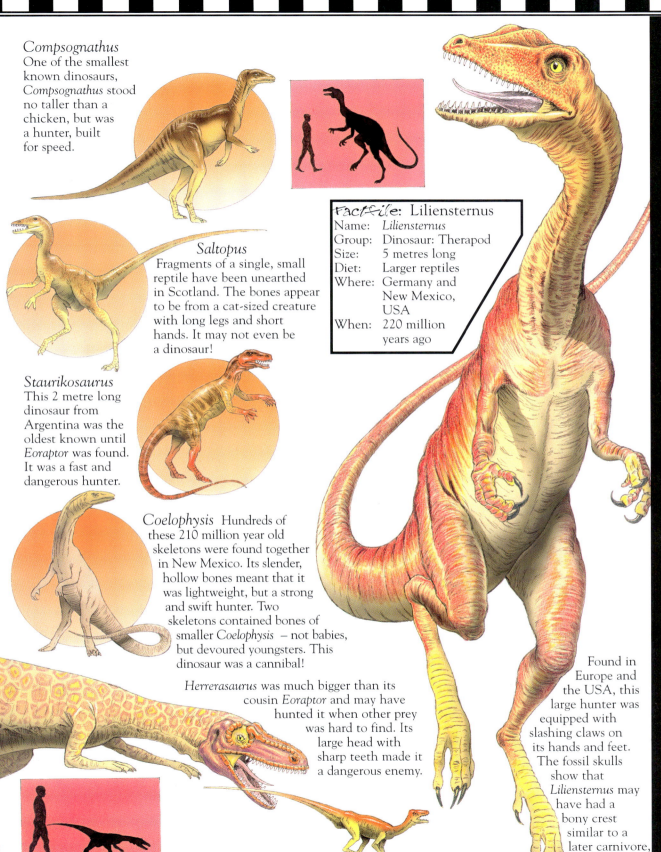

Compsognathus
One of the smallest known dinosaurs, *Compsognathus* stood no taller than a chicken, but was a hunter, built for speed.

Saltopus
Fragments of a single, small reptile have been unearthed in Scotland. The bones appear to be from a cat-sized creature with long legs and short hands. It may not even be a dinosaur!

Staurikosaurus
This 2 metre long dinosaur from Argentina was the oldest known until *Eoraptor* was found. It was a fast and dangerous hunter.

Factfile: Liliensternus
Name: *Liliensternus*
Group: Dinosaur: Therapod
Size: 5 metres long
Diet: Larger reptiles
Where: Germany and New Mexico, USA
When: 220 million years ago

Coelophysis Hundreds of these 210 million year old skeletons were found together in New Mexico. Its slender, hollow bones meant that it was lightweight, but a strong and swift hunter. Two skeletons contained bones of smaller *Coelophysis* – not babies, but devoured youngsters. This dinosaur was a cannibal!

Herrerasaurus was much bigger than its cousin *Eoraptor* and may have hunted it when other prey was hard to find. Its large head with sharp teeth made it a dangerous enemy.

Found in Europe and the USA, this large hunter was equipped with slashing claws on its hands and feet. The fossil skulls show that *Liliensternus* may have had a bony crest similar to a later carnivore, *Dilophosaurus*.

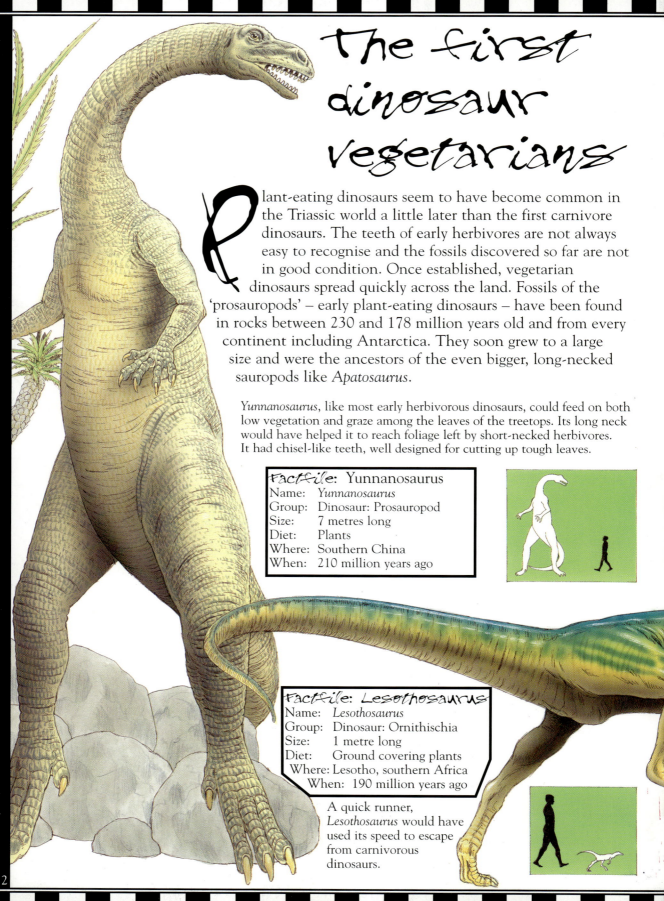

The first dinosaur vegetarians

Plant-eating dinosaurs seem to have become common in the Triassic world a little later than the first carnivore dinosaurs. The teeth of early herbivores are not always easy to recognise and the fossils discovered so far are not in good condition. Once established, vegetarian dinosaurs spread quickly across the land. Fossils of the 'prosauropods' – early plant-eating dinosaurs – have been found in rocks between 230 and 178 million years old and from every continent including Antarctica. They soon grew to a large size and were the ancestors of the even bigger, long-necked sauropods like *Apatosaurus*.

Yunnanosaurus, like most early herbivorous dinosaurs, could feed on both low vegetation and graze among the leaves of the treetops. Its long neck would have helped it to reach foliage left by short-necked herbivores. It had chisel-like teeth, well designed for cutting up tough leaves.

Factfile: Yunnanosaurus
Name: *Yunnanosaurus*
Group: Dinosaur: Prosauropod
Size: 7 metres long
Diet: Plants
Where: Southern China
When: 210 million years ago

Factfile: Lesothosaurus
Name: *Lesothosaurus*
Group: Dinosaur: Ornithischia
Size: 1 metre long
Diet: Ground covering plants
Where: Lesotho, southern Africa
When: 190 million years ago

A quick runner, *Lesothosaurus* would have used its speed to escape from carnivorous dinosaurs.

Pisanosaurus measured less than 1 metre long and was one of the very first herbivorous dinosaurs. It is known only from a single fragmented skull and skeleton found in Argentina.

Plateosaurus' jaws contained dozens of small, leaf-shaped teeth ideal for shredding food, but not for chewing.

Plateosaurus had a defensive thumb claw to make up for its lack of speed.

FactFile: Plateosaurus

Name: *Plateosaurus*
Group: Dinosaur: Prosauropod
Size: 6-8 metres long
Diet: Plants
Where: Europe (England, France, Germany and Switzerland)
When: 210 million years ago

Lufengosaurus was a close cousin to *Yunnanosaurus*, *Plateosaurus* and *Coloradisaurus*.

Like all herbivorous dinosaurs, *Lufengosaurus* probably had stones (gastroliths) in its stomach to help grind the tough plant food into a more digestible form.

FactFile: Lufengosaurus

Name: *Lufengosaurus*
Group: Dinosaur: Prosauropod
Size: 6 metres long
Diet: Plants
Where: Southern China
When: 200 million years ago

The first dinosaur vegetarians

Big dinosaurs

In the Jurassic Period (213-144 million years ago) the world in which the dinosaurs lived saw many changes. The continents split apart and the climate became cooler and wetter, bringing moist tropical conditions to most parts of the Earth. Certain plants, especially ferns and conifers, became widespread and provided much better food for the herbivorous dinosaurs than the older types of vegetation. New dinosaurs began to exploit this banquet of foliage and the long-necked, long-tailed sauropods soon became the largest animals ever to walk on land. They weighed between 30 and 80 tonnes and perhaps even as much as 130 tonnes! Their large size made them safe from most smaller predators, and a steady body temperature meant more efficient use of energy. Increased size meant that walking on four feet became necessary, especially since such huge dinosaurs needed huge stomachs and massive amounts of food.

Factfile : Brachiosaurus
Name: *Brachiosaurus*
Group: Dinosaur: Sauropod
Size: 23 metres long, 12 metres high
Diet: Tree leaves and shoots
Where: Tanzania, east Africa;
        Algeria, north Africa
        and western USA
When: 152-145 million
        years ago

Together with its long neck and strong jaws, *Brachiosaurus* was superbly equipped for feeding among the treetops.

From the remains of five dinosaurs found in Tanzania, the largest dinosaur skeleton ever was assembled. Its legs bore a huge body, with the front legs longer than the hindlegs.

The remarkable neck of *Mamenchisaurus* was strengthened by a system of spines underneath the vertebrae. As a result the neck was inflexible and probably could not be lifted to a great height. It perhaps fed on low-lying vegetation, grazing as it swept its head from side to side.

Factfile: Mamenchisaurus
Name: *Mamenchisaurus*
Group: Dinosaur: Sauropod
Size: 22 metres long, 5 metres high
Diet: Plants
Where: Sichuan, China
When: 145 million years ago

Factfile: Seismosaurus

Name:	*Seismosaurus*
Group:	Dinosaur: Sauropod
Size:	38-52 metres long, 3.5 metres high
Diet:	Plants
Where:	Western USA
When:	120 million years ago

Though the skull of *Seismosaurus* has not yet been discovered, it is believed to be rather small.

Enormous hip and back bones were discovered in New Mexico in 1979. The back vertebrae above the hips were fused together to form an immensely strong beam which bridged the hindlegs.

Strong tendons and muscles above the neck bones were anchored to each vertebrae and then back to the shoulders.

The shoulders and backs of sauropods form an arch. When mounted on four pillar-like legs, the whole structure is very strong and stable.

As well as having muscular stomachs, *Seismosaurus* swallowed stones which helped to grind down rough plant food. More than 240 of these gastroliths were found when skeletons were first excavated. The largest was 10 centimetres across.

Sauropods could be surprisingly slim. This would be an advantage when walking through heavily wooded areas in search of food.

The necks of sauropods contained 12 to 15 vertebrae, with *Mamenchisaurus* having as many as 19. Each vertebra was elongated as in a modern giraffe. Their light structure provided minimum weight with maximum strength.

The feet of *Seismosaurus* and other sauropods were like an elephant's. There were five short toes on each foot. The thumb of each front foot and three of the toes on each foot had claws.

Ferocious dinosaurs

Of all the dinosaurs known to have existed, none capture the imagination as much as the huge meat-eating dinosaurs. From their beginnings as the fierce but small hunters in the Triassic Period, they developed into the terrifying killing machines which preyed on the grazing herbivores in the Jurassic, and later, Cretaceous Periods. Armed with ferocious teeth set in the powerful jaws of enormous heads, they could overcome just about any other animal. Only the largest sauropods may have escaped being their prey.

Factfile: Tyrannosaurus
Name: *Tyrannosaurus*
Group: Dinosaur: Carnosaur
Size: 13 metres long
Diet: Reptiles, dead or alive
Where: North America, China
        and Mongolia
When: 70-65 million years ago

Tyrannosaurus rex is perhaps the most famous of all dinosaurs. It was one of the last to have existed. Though the function of the 15 centimetre long teeth is clear, scientists still puzzle over the value of the tiny arms which didn't even reach its mouth!

Found recently in the deserts of the Sahara, the mighty *Carcharodontosaurus* puts even *Tyrannosaurus* in the shade.

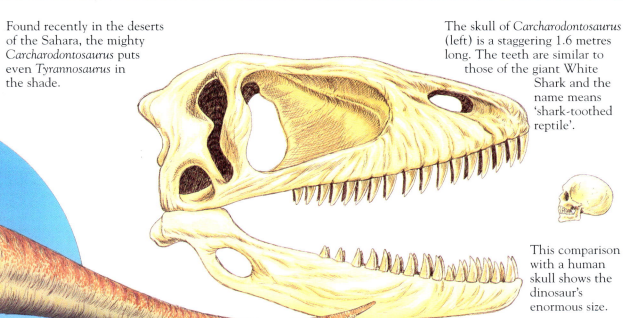

The skull of *Carcharodontosaurus* (left) is a staggering 1.6 metres long. The teeth are similar to those of the giant White Shark and the name means 'shark-toothed reptile'.

This comparison with a human skull shows the dinosaur's enormous size.

Factfile: Carcharodontosaurus

Name:	*Carcharodontosaurus*
Group:	Dinosaur: Carnosaur
Size:	12 metres long
Diet:	Reptiles
Where:	Morocco, North Africa
When:	90 million years ago

Below, a *Tyrannosaurus rex* is chasing the sauropod *Alamosaurus* into a lake.

Some scientists believe that *T. rex* was a fast runner and deadly hunter. Others claim that it was a slow runner and think that it fed on dead or dying dinosaurs, rather like a vulture. Its braincase holds evidence that it had a very good sense of smell. So this scene may or may not have been possible.

Deadly enemies

razing herbivorous dinosaurs would constantly check for the presence of hunting carnivores. Like zebras or gazelles today, many species would graze in herds, as there is safety in numbers. For the gentle giants like *Mamenchisaurus* sheer size might put off an attack from even the largest *Tyrannosaurus*. For others, defensive weapons and armour-plating evolved to provide some protection from physical attack. A wide variety of horns and spikes, clubbed tails and claws have been found as fossils. But defence was not only needed against carnivores. Like modern deer, elephants and rhinoceros, rival male dinosaurs would fight for the leadership of herds and for supremacy in mating.

Styracosaurus lived about 80 million years ago in North America. The frill of the largest male would have frightened off rivals while its single horn was a deadly weapon.

The *Centrosaurus*'s central horn was surrounded by a frill with bumps around the edge.

Factfile:
Triceratops
Name:	*Triceratops*
Group:	Dinosaur: Ceratopsia
Size:	9 metres long
Diet:	Plants
Where:	North America
When:	70-65 million years ago

Each of the three massive horns from which this dinosaur gets its name would have been covered with a tough, sharp sheath made of a similar substance to human fingernails, providing very impressive weapons. The neck was well protected by a solid bony covering or frill.

More than 50 skulls of the herbivorous *Triceratops* have been found. They vary in shape but measure up to 1.2 metres long.

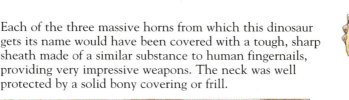

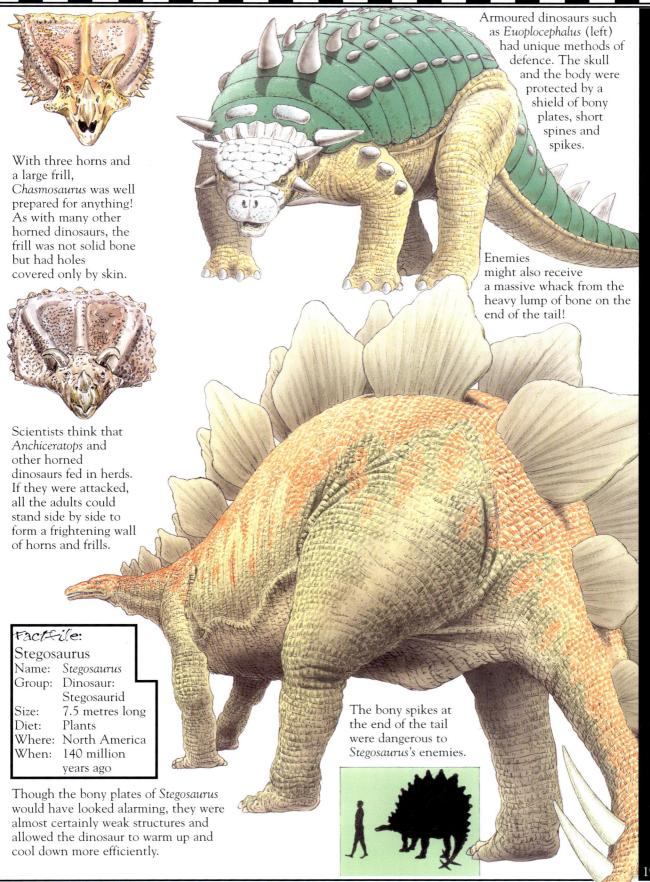

Armoured dinosaurs such as *Euoplocephalus* (left) had unique methods of defence. The skull and the body were protected by a shield of bony plates, short spines and spikes.

With three horns and a large frill, *Chasmosaurus* was well prepared for anything! As with many other horned dinosaurs, the frill was not solid bone but had holes covered only by skin.

Scientists think that *Anchiceratops* and other horned dinosaurs fed in herds. If they were attacked, all the adults could stand side by side to form a frightening wall of horns and frills.

Enemies might also receive a massive whack from the heavy lump of bone on the end of the tail!

Factfile:
Stegosaurus
Name: *Stegosaurus*
Group: Dinosaur: Stegosaurid
Size: 7.5 metres long
Diet: Plants
Where: North America
When: 140 million years ago

Though the bony plates of *Stegosaurus* would have looked alarming, they were almost certainly weak structures and allowed the dinosaur to warm up and cool down more efficiently.

The bony spikes at the end of the tail were dangerous to *Stegosaurus*'s enemies.

Eggs, nests and dinosaur young

Most types of dinosaur are believed to have laid eggs. All known dinosaur eggs had hard shells like birds' eggs. Egg remains have been found all over the world, most famously in the Gobi Desert of Mongolia and 'Egg Mountain' in Montana, USA. Identifying which dinosaur laid which egg is difficult, unless skeletons of young dinosaurs are found very close to eggshell remains. Rarely, eggs are discovered in which the bones of the embryo dinosaur still exist. We know that at least some dinosaurs made nests. A clutch of 24 eggs laid by the small carnivore *Troodon* was found in Montana surrounded by a 12 centimetre high rim of mud. A skeleton of *Oviraptor* was found in Mongolia still sitting on its eggs!

Large groups of *Maiasaura*, a herbivorous dinosaur, laid eggs in colonies of nests between 90 and 65 million years ago.

Each nest was positioned so that the parent caring for one nest could not interfere with any other chick or parent. The nest was made out of soil and vegetation.

Maiasaura eggs were laid in batches of a dozen or so. Each was about 12 centimetres long and roughly spherical. Despite the enormous size of some dinosaurs, the dinosaur young could never have hatched from enormous eggs. The shells would have been too thick to break and would not have allowed oxygen to pass through the shell.

Maiasaura probably brought food to the nests (right), just as parent birds do for chicks today.

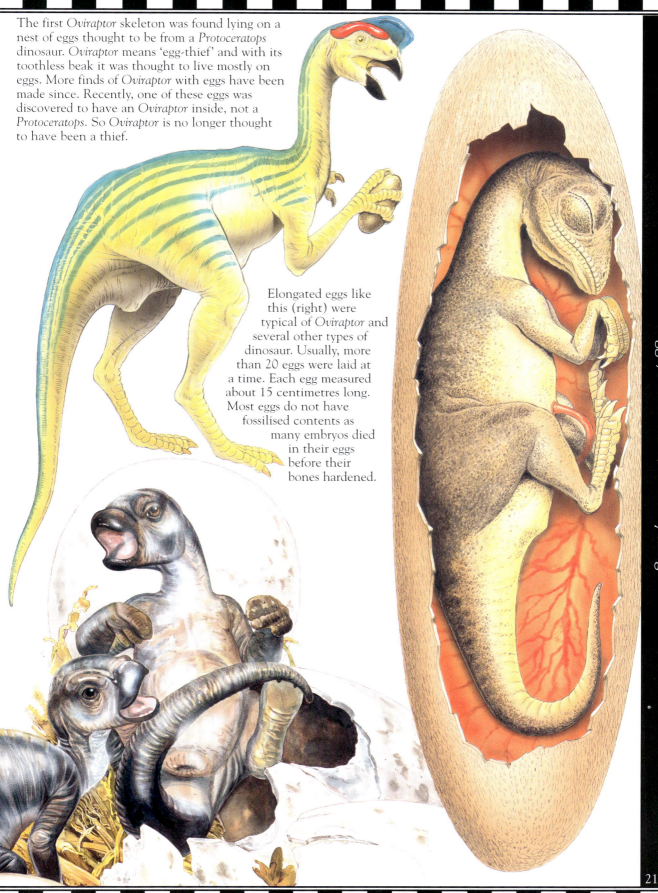

The first *Oviraptor* skeleton was found lying on a nest of eggs thought to be from a *Protoceratops* dinosaur. *Oviraptor* means 'egg-thief' and with its toothless beak it was thought to live mostly on eggs. More finds of *Oviraptor* with eggs have been made since. Recently, one of these eggs was discovered to have an *Oviraptor* inside, not a *Protoceratops*. So *Oviraptor* is no longer thought to have been a thief.

Elongated eggs like this (right) were typical of *Oviraptor* and several other types of dinosaur. Usually, more than 20 eggs were laid at a time. Each egg measured about 15 centimetres long. Most eggs do not have fossilised contents as many embryos died in their eggs before their bones hardened.

Tracking dinosaurs

A herd of *Brachiosaurus* strolling along the muddy shore of a lake in Texas would have had no idea that the footprints they left behind would still be around 80 million years later. In fact, dinosaur footprints give us clues which are impossible to discover from fossil bones, teeth or eggs. Made by the living animals, footprints can tell us a lot about the day to day activities of dinosaurs. Fossil footprints are surprisingly common. They come in all shapes and sizes from chicken-sized prints to enormous sauropod prints, three times larger than those of elephants. They have been found in thousands of places on all the continents except Antarctica. Some footprints are found a few at a time, some in millions across thousands of square kilometres. They were probably made by animals crossing beaches, tidal flats and lagoons near coasts, swamps, rivers and lake shorelines.

Carnivorous therapod dinosaurs like *Allosaurus* were bipedal (two-footed) and had well-equipped feet with sharp claws. These were useful weapons for capturing and killing prey. Therapods usually walked 'pigeon-toed' and with one foot placed in front of the other.

Corythosaurus was one of the hadrosaurs or 'duck-billed' dinosaurs. Like many bipedal herbivorous dinosaurs each foot had three toes and, instead of claws, each toe ended in a blunt sort of hoof. Such feet were useful equipment for escaping from the attentions of a predator!

The feet of sauropods like *Apatosaurus* had to carry their enormous weight. Each foot was a large rounded pad with the toes splayed out to help spread the load. The inner toe of each foot carried an especially long claw, useful for self-defence or gripping branches when feeding.

The distance between footprints can be measured and the speed calculated. *Albertosaursus* may have run as fast as 45 km per hour.

Iguanodon probably walked on its hindlegs most of the time but fed on all fours to reach low-lying plants. Its large hind feet made big three-toed prints and its forefeet made small horse-shoe shaped prints. A left footprint is clearly different to a right footprint.

Aprons worn when performing the Hopi Indian Snake Dance (left) include dinosaur footprints in the design, showing that dinosaur tracks were discovered by North American Indians long before scientists.

Deep sauropod footprints in Colorado, USA (right) provide natural paddling pools and give a useful idea of scale when compared to a small boy!

The 'thumb' of each *Iguanodon* hand was a sharp spike which could not touch the other fingers, but stuck out. It was almost certainly a defensive weapon which could be used to slash at attacking carnivores.

Iguanodon is one of a large group of related dinosaurs which have been found across the world. Its chest contains an unusual bone which may have helped to strengthen it and assisted the dinosaur to walk on all fours.

With short front legs and long hindlegs, *Iguanodon* was in danger of falling forwards when on all fours! To prevent this, it had a thick, muscular tail which had stiffening rods of bony tendons running along it. This balanced the dinosaur from the hips.

Factfile: Iguanodon

Name: *Iguanodon*
Group: Dinosaur: Ornithopoda
Size: 9 metres long
Diet: Plants
Where: Europe, North America and Mongolia
When: 120-110 million years ago

The middle three fingers of each forefoot are nearly joined and slightly spread out. If the *Iguanodon* regularly used its hands for walking they may have been covered in a tough mitten-like pad of skin.

The last of the dinosaurs

The last of the three geological periods in which the dinosaurs lived was the Cretaceous. It lasted from 145 to 65 million years ago. About half of all known dinosaurs lived during this period. The Earth's climate was warm for much of that time. Many modern forms of life started to become common – mammals, birds, snakes, insects, flowering plants and broad-leafed trees flourished. Towards the end of the period, the global temperature began to fall. This cooling had an effect on the numbers of different types of plants and animals living at that time. Dinosaurs changed too. There were fewer large sauropods, the horned dinosaurs and duck-billed hadrosaurs became more common and the curious 'thick-headed' dinosaurs evolved. *Tyrannosaurus rex* and its cousins ruled the carnivores.

The single huge landmass changed during the Cretaceous Period. The continents drifted apart and were divided by large seas. This affected the climate.

Factfile: Parasaurolophus
Name: *Parasaurolophus*
Group: Dinosaur: Hadrosaur
Size: 10 metres long
Diet: Plants
Where: Western North America
When: 80-65 million years ago

Along the old Cretaceous shores of the western USA and Canada there are many places where masses of hadrosaur bones have been found. It seems that now and then, large numbers of these dinosaurs died together, perhaps because of a flood. But why were they in such large groups? The best explanation is that hadrosaurs had learnt to migrate, to move south for the winter to find more supplies of food, but we may never know for sure.

Several types of 'duck-billed' dinosaurs had strange bony crests on their skulls (see below). They contained hollow bony passages which were joined to the nostrils. It seems likely that these crests were used like the tubes of a trumpet and could produce loud honking noises for display or threat.

The first bird we know of was *Archaeopteryx*, which lived 150 million years ago. Scientists now widely believe that birds evolved from small carnivorous dinosaurs. By the end of the Cretaceous Period, most of the modern groups of birds had appeared. *Presbyornis* is an early duck from Europe, USA and South America. *Ichthyornis* from the USA had teeth in its beak and probably fed on fish.

Factfile: Pachycephalosaurus

Name: *Pachycephalosaurus*
Group: Dinosaur: Ornithischia
Size: 8 metres long
Diet: Various plants
Where: Western North America
When: 70-65 million years ago

Many types of 'thick-headed' dinosaurs had evolved and lived not only in North America but also in Mongolia, Europe and China. *Pachycephalosaurus* was the largest. The thickened skulls were probably used for fighting between competing dinosaurs. Some skulls are thicker than others – these probably belonged to the male animals.

The skulls of the 'thick-headed' dinosaurs, like *Pachycephalosaurus*, were reinforced with up to 22 centimetres of bone on the top.

The end of the dinosaurs

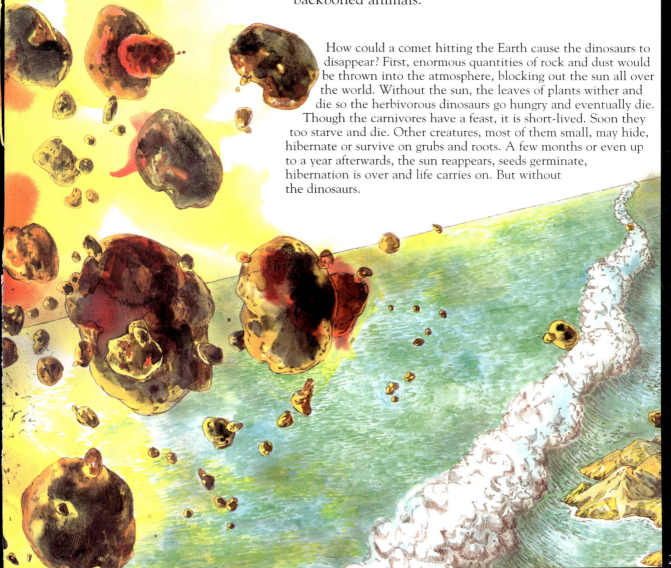

Under the floor of the Caribbean Sea, off the northern tip of the Yucatan Peninsula in Mexico, there is a circular crater 177 kilometres wide. This is the best evidence yet of a gigantic explosion – the impact of an estimated 15 kilometre-wide comet hitting the Earth about 65 million years ago. It may also answer the question: why did the dinosaurs die out? Did the comet cause the dinosaurs to disappear? Well, maybe. Scientists are far from sure because other things were happening to the Earth at the same time. Seas had invaded the land everywhere, wiping out former coastlines, so there were fewer places for dinosaurs to live. In India and Pakistan, huge volcanoes pumped out hundreds of thousands of cubic kilometres of lava. This would have had a significant effect on the climate. Perhaps all three things combined caused not only the end of the dinosaurs, but also many other species – perhaps half of all known backboned animals.

How could a comet hitting the Earth cause the dinosaurs to disappear? First, enormous quantities of rock and dust would be thrown into the atmosphere, blocking out the sun all over the world. Without the sun, the leaves of plants wither and die so the herbivorous dinosaurs go hungry and eventually die. Though the carnivores have a feast, it is short-lived. Soon they too starve and die. Other creatures, most of them small, may hide, hibernate or survive on grubs and roots. A few months or even up to a year afterwards, the sun reappears, seeds germinate, hibernation is over and life carries on. But without the dinosaurs.

History mystery?

The smallest of the neck vertebrae is positioned near the skull, which is the last part of the replica to be added.

These days none of the dinosaur skeletons in museum displays are made from real bones. The original fossils are too heavy to support and they are always in danger of collapse or damage. Such valuable specimens cannot be risked. Instead, replica bones are made out of fibreglass or resin and are very lightweight. In this way, even a full-size skeleton needs little support and looks as natural as possible. However, producing a replica dinosaur skeleton is a very difficult job and hugely expensive.

Dinosaur hunting is carefully planned. Firstly, rocks which might contain dinosaur fossils have to be found. They have to be the right age, laid down during the time when dinosaurs lived. They must be the right type, deposited in layers by rivers or lakes, in deserts or near swamps and lagoons. Fossil hunters search where rocks appear on the surface – on cliffs and in quarries, high up mountains or in hot, barren landscapes. In these places, experienced eyes search for clues that dinosaurs were in the neighbourhood, such as fossils of the plants that the dinosaurs fed on or fish and shellfish fossils from the lakes where they gathered to drink. With luck, a bone will be seen sticking out from a layer of rock and maybe, just maybe, the rest of the skeleton lies beneath. Then the hard work really begins.

A fossilised bone is found and exposed by scraping away the surrounding rocks. Photographs and drawings are done.

As the bone dries in the air it may need to be painted with resin to protect the fragile and cracked surface.

Rock is slowly cleared away from the sides of the bone until it is supported only by a narrow pillar of rock.

The bone is covered in wet tissue and strips of plaster bandage. This hardens and protects the fossil.

As much of the bone is covered in plaster as possible. The bone is removed from the ground, and the rest is covered in plaster.

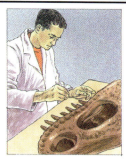

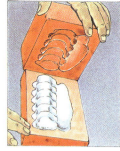

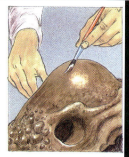

The bones are taken to a museum, where the plaster jackets are cut away and the bones uncovered. Any remaining rock is removed and the bone is carefully cleaned.

More delicate work is possible in a laboratory. The lighting is good, specialized tools are available and the use of microscopes allows the finest of repairs.

Once scientists have identified all the bones, they begin to work with artists who illustrate how they might join together and what the dinosaur would have looked like when it was alive.

The bones are used to produce moulds in rubber from which replicas are made. The delicate originals are then handled less often and copies can be sent around the world for study.

The copies are carefully painted so that they exactly match the appearance of the original bones. Replicas are usually used for museum displays so the originals can be kept safely in storage.

The neck vertebrae are added once those from the shoulders to hips are in position. The largest of the neck bones is placed near the shoulders.

The vertebrae from shoulder to hip are threaded onto a carefully bent rod of steel which is then fixed to two supports between the front and back legs.

The legs are also threaded onto steel supports which are then hung from the central rod together with the ribs.

The tail vertebrae are threaded onto the steel rod in order: largest first, smallest last.

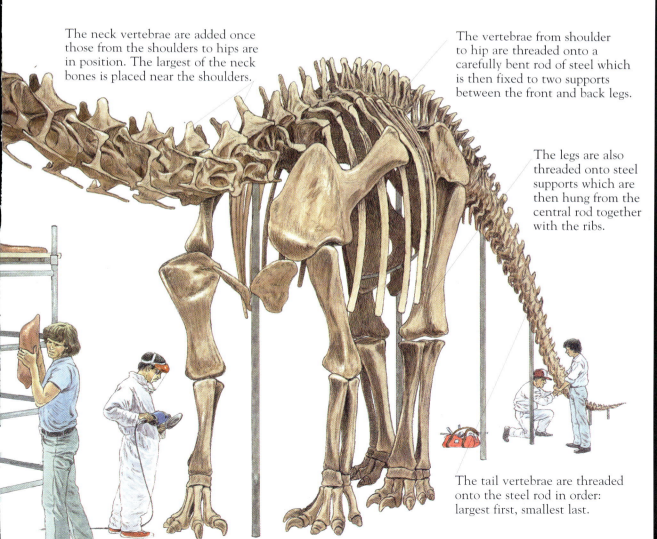

Dinosaur quiz

1. What is the world's oldest known dinosaur called?
a) Eoraptor
b) Lagosuchus
c) Dimetrodon

2. At least one dinosaur seems to have become a cannibal. Which one was it?
a) Herrerasaurus
b) Composognathus
c) Coelophysis

3. Prosauropods were early types of which kind of dinosaur?
a) Herbivorous
b) Carnivorous
c) Armoured dinosaurs.

4. Where was the dinosaur Mamenchisaurus found?
a) North America
b) China
c) South America

5. Hundreds of dinosaur eggs have been found on 'Egg Mountain'. In which country were they discovered?
a) Mongolia
b) Canada
c) United States of America

6. What unusual weapon did Iguanodon have?
a) A tail spine.
b) A thumb spike.
c) A horn.

7. What was the long bony crest of Parasaurolophus used for?
a) Making mating calls or threatening noises.
b) As a defensive weapon.
c) As a snorkel.

8. What does Triceratops get its name from?
a) Its three toes on each foot.
b) The three frills around its neck.
c) The three horns on its head.

9. In which geological period of time did the dinosaurs live?
a) The Palaeozoic period.
b) The Mesozoic period.
c) The Cenozoic period.

10. What is the first known bird called?
a) Archaeopteryx
b) Presbyornis
c) Protoceratops

Quiz answers are on page 32.

Glossary

ancestor An early form of animal or plant from which others have developed, usually with a very long time between forms.

bipedal Standing or walking on two legs. Walking on all fours is known as quadrupedal.

carnivore Any animal that eats the flesh of other animals as its main food source.

carnosaur A group of large carnivore dinosaurs with huge skulls and enormous teeth, such as *Tyrannosaurus*.

Ceratopsia A group of dinosaurs that included all the horned dinosaurs from the late Cretaceous period, such as *Triceratops*.

comet An object in the solar system that travels around the sun and is made of ice and rocks. The frozen material evaporates as it nears the sun and forms the comet's tail.

conifer One of a large group of mostly evergreen cone-bearing trees such as firs and pines.

Cretaceous The geological time period that began about 145 million years ago and ended about 65 million years ago.

embryo The young of an animal that develops within an egg or womb.

fern A type of plant that first appeared over 400 million years ago and formed a major food source for herbivorous dinosaurs.

gastrolith A stone or pebble, swallowed by an animal and kept in its gut. Gastroliths help to grind up food which is difficult to digest.

germinate The moment that a seed begins to sprout a root and shoot.

hadrosaur One of a group of large herbivorous dinosaurs that lived during the late Cretaceous period and which often had bony skull crests and duck-billed jaws. Parasaurolophus was a hadrosaur.

herbivore Any animal that eats plant material as its major food source.

Jurassic The geological time period that began about 213 million years ago and ended about 144 million years ago.

Mesozoic A major division of geological time known as an Era which included the Triassic, Jurassic and Cretaceous periods. It lasted from 248 million years ago until 65 million years ago.

ornithischia A group of dinosaurs all of which had a hip structure similar to birds, such as Lesothosaurus. These dinosaurs were all herbivorous.

Ornithopoda Group of ornithischian dinosaurs that generally walked on two legs and three-toed feet such as *Iguanadon*.

pelycosaur A group of early reptiles that developed about 300 million years ago. It is believed that they were the ancestors of mammals.

plesiosaur A large swimming reptile that lived in the seas and oceans during the Mesozoic era.

predator Any animal that hunts and then eats another animal.

prosauropod A member of a group of dinosaurs that lived during the Triassic and Jurassic periods and which were among the first of the large herbivorous dinosaur.

pterodactyl A flying reptile or pterosaur that lived during the Jurassic and Cretaceous periods. Pterodactyls all had short tails.

pterosaur A flying reptile that first appeared during the Triassic period. This group includes the pterodactyls.

saurischians Group of dinosaurs all of which had hip structures similar to lizards.

sauropod One of a group of very large, herbivorous and quadrupedal dinosaurs such as *Diplodocus*, *Apatosaurus* and *Mamenchisaurus*.

stegosaurid A dinosaur that belongs to the group which includes *Stegosaurus*, all of which have one or two rows of bony plates or spines along the back. They lived during the Cretaceous and Jurassic periods.

thecodontian An early reptile that lived more than 250 million years ago. The thecodontians were the ancestors of dinosaurs, crocodiles and pterosaurs.

therapod A therapod dinosaur was a carnivore with the saurischian or 'lizard-hipped' form of hip such as *Compsognathus*.

Triassic The geological time period that lasted from 248 million years ago to 213 million years ago.

vertebra One of the many complicated bones that make up the spine or vertebral column of all back-boned animals.

Index